Seymour Public Library
46 Church Street
Seymour, CT 06483

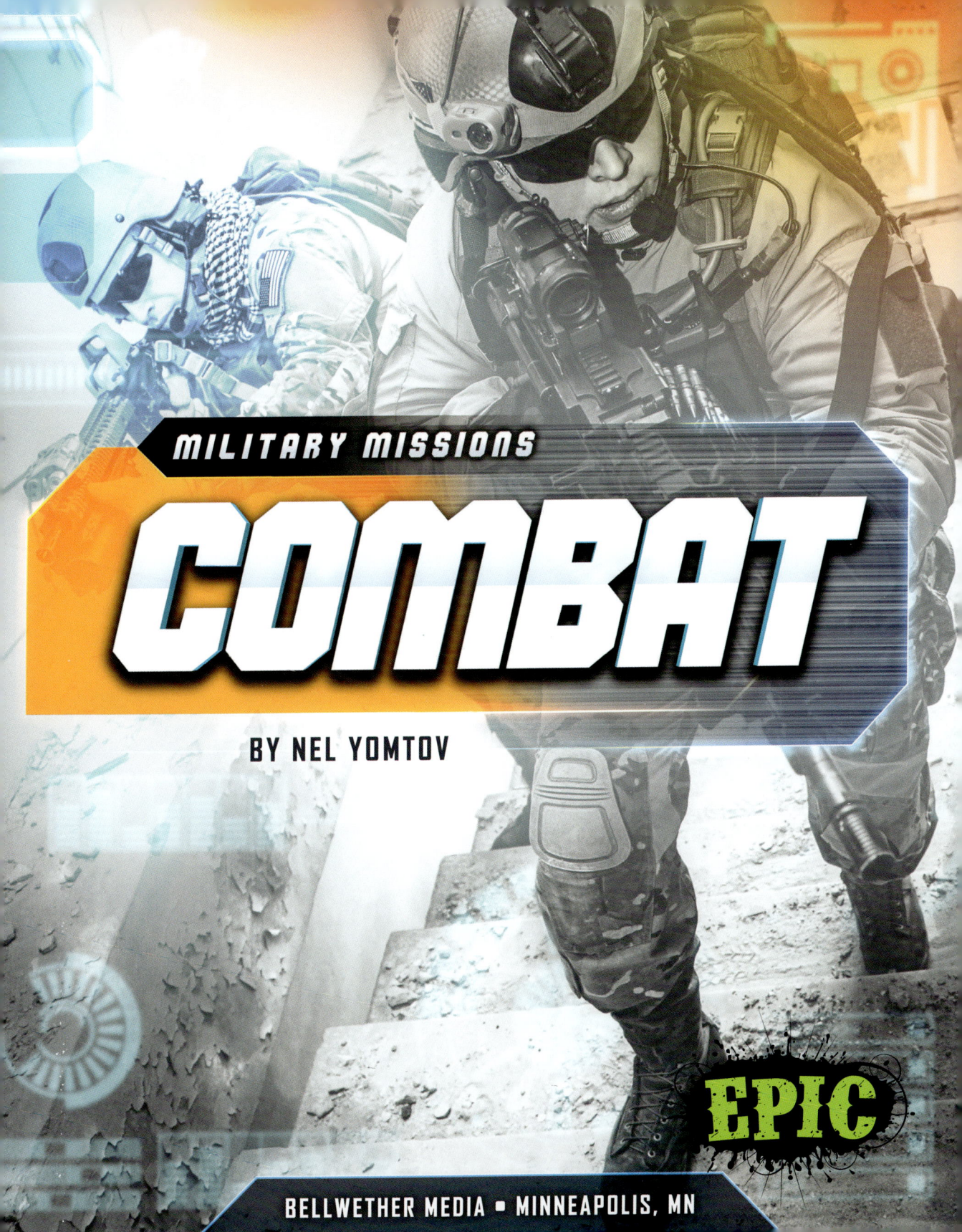

MILITARY MISSIONS

COMBAT

BY NEL YOMTOV

EPIC

BELLWETHER MEDIA • MINNEAPOLIS, MN

EPIC

EPIC BOOKS are no ordinary books. They burst with intense action, high-speed heroics, and shadows of the unknown. Are you ready for an Epic adventure?

This edition first published in 2017 by Bellwether Media, Inc.

No part of this publication may be reproduced in whole or in part without written permission of the publisher.
For information regarding permission, write to Bellwether Media, Inc., Attention: Permissions Department, 5357 Penn Avenue South, Minneapolis, MN 55419.

Library of Congress Cataloging-in-Publication Data

Names: Yomtov, Nelson, author.
Title: Combat / by Nel Yomtov.
Description: Minneapolis, MN : Bellwether Media, Inc., 2017. | Series: Epic:
  Military Missions | Includes bibliographical references and index. |
  Audience: Grades 2-7.
Identifiers: LCCN 2015050474 | ISBN 9781626174337 (hardcover :
  alk. paper)
Subjects: LCSH: United States. Army. Special Forces–Juvenile literature. |
  Combat–Juvenile literature. | Iraq War, 2003-2011–Juvenile literature
Classification: LCC UA34.S64 Y67 2017 | DDC 355.4/73–dc23
LC record available at http://lccn.loc.gov/2015050474

Text copyright © 2017 by Bellwether Media, Inc. EPIC and associated logos are trademarks and/or registered trademarks of Bellwether Media, Inc. SCHOLASTIC, CHILDREN'S PRESS, and associated logos are trademarks and/or registered trademarks of Scholastic Inc.

Printed in the United States of America, North Mankato, MN.

TABLE OF CONTENTS

Under Attack!	4
The Mission	8
The Plan	12
The Team	16
Accomplished!	20
Glossary	22
To Learn More	23
Index	24

UNDER ATTACK!

Loud gun blasts sound. A team of **Green Berets** is under attack in Iraq. The United States Army sent the group to take an important road from the enemy.

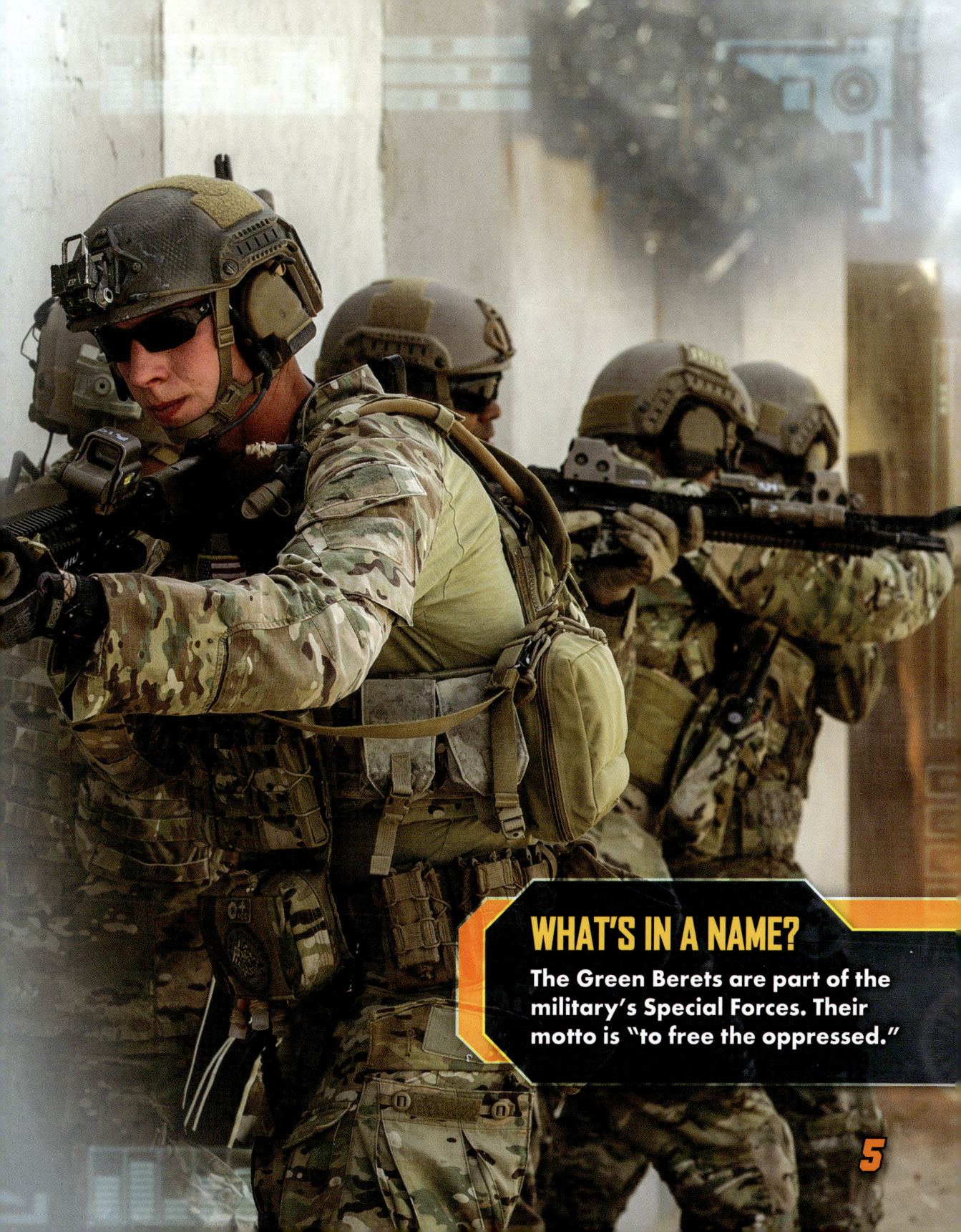

WHAT'S IN A NAME?

The Green Berets are part of the military's Special Forces. Their motto is "to free the oppressed."

The Green Berets are **outnumbered**. But that does not stop them. They fire back at the enemy.

Hours later, the enemy gives up. The Americans take control of the road!

A PRESIDENTIAL ORDER
President John F. Kennedy helped name the Green Berets. He made the beret the group's official hat.

THE MISSION

Soldiers are sent on combat missions to fight enemy forces. Sometimes they fight to save lives. They may capture the enemy's land or supplies.

Combat troops are often on the move. They gather **intelligence** about the enemy or the land. They get into the best position to fight.

REAL-LIFE COMBAT

What: Battle of Midway
Who: United States military vs. Japanese military
Where: Midway Islands, Pacific Ocean
When: June 3–7, 1942, during World War II
Why: Fought for control of the Pacific Ocean
How: Americans sank 5 Japanese ships, including 4 aircraft carriers, and destroyed more than 300 aircraft

United States planes aboard the USS *Enterprise*

THE PLAN

During a battle, soldiers often carry guns called M4 **carbines**. Powerful MP5 **machine guns** are used, too.

M4 carbine

missile

DRESS SMART
Safety gear is needed for battle. Helmets and body armor protect soldiers from enemy fire.

Soldiers also fire **missiles**. These weapons can destroy big **armored** vehicles.

13

Fighter jets and **bombers** fire weapons from high in the sky. Other aircraft sometimes bring troops to battle.

B-1B Lancer bomber

F-35A Lightning II fighter jet

A LOT OF GAS!
The U.S. military uses more than 12 million gallons (45 million liters) of fuel each day.

Helicopters can **hover** while soldiers slide down ropes. Some soldiers **parachute** from airplanes!

THE TEAM

U.S. combat forces can fight anywhere. The Army and Marines often carry out their work on the ground.

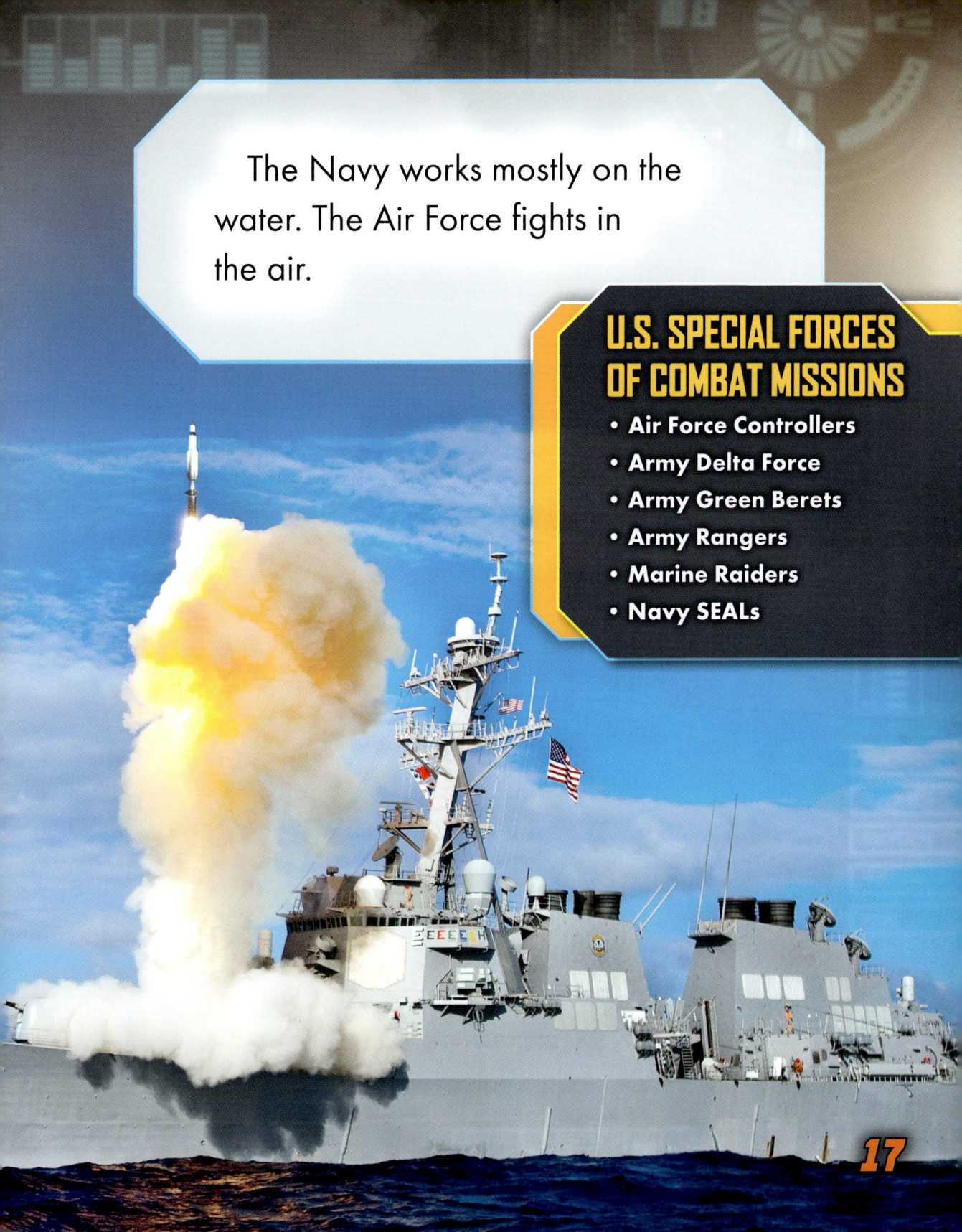

The Navy works mostly on the water. The Air Force fights in the air.

U.S. SPECIAL FORCES OF COMBAT MISSIONS

- Air Force Controllers
- Army Delta Force
- Army Green Berets
- Army Rangers
- Marine Raiders
- Navy SEALs

Soldiers learn how to fight at **basic training**. But combat can require other skills, too.

Some soldiers learn to dive underwater to destroy enemy ships. Others learn **foreign** languages to work in distant countries.

SOLDIER PROFILE

For combat missions, a soldier must have:
- Courage
- Self-confidence
- Excellent physical fitness
- Loyalty
- Sense of duty
- Intelligence

ACCOMPLISHED!

Combat missions are carefully planned. Each one has a clear purpose. When a mission is over, soldiers rest and prepare for the next one!

GLOSSARY

armored—covered in thick plates for protection

basic training—the beginning of military training that includes teaching basic combat skills

bombers—large military aircraft that drop bombs on targets

carbines—long, lightweight guns

foreign—related to another country or place

Green Berets—specially trained soldiers in the United States Army Special Forces

hover—to stay in one spot while in flight

intelligence—information about an enemy's position, movements, or weapons

machine guns—automatic weapons that rapidly fire bullets

missiles—explosives that are sent to targets

outnumbered—to have fewer people than another group

parachute—to jump from an aircraft with a parachute; a parachute is a large, umbrella-shaped cloth attached to someone to help them fall safely from the air.

TO LEARN MORE

AT THE LIBRARY

Callery, Sean. *Branches of the Military*. New York, N.Y.: Scholastic, Inc., 2015.

Labrecque, Ellen. *Special Forces*. Chicago, Ill.: Raintree, 2012.

Markovics, Joyce. *Today's Army Heroes*. New York, N.Y.: Bearport Pub., 2012.

ON THE WEB

Learning more about combat is as easy as 1, 2, 3.

1. Go to www.factsurfer.com.

2. Enter "combat" into the search box.

3. Click the "Surf" button and you will see a list of related web sites.

With factsurfer.com, finding more information is just a click away.

INDEX

airplanes, 15
armored vehicles, 13
basic training, 18
bombers, 14
capture, 8
carbines, 12
dive, 18
enemy, 4, 7, 8, 10, 13, 18
fighter jets, 14
foreign languages, 18
fuel, 15
Green Berets, 4, 5, 7
helicopters, 15
intelligence, 10
Iraq, 4

Kennedy, John F. (president), 7
machine guns, 12
Marines, 16, 17
missiles, 13
missions, 8, 19, 20
parachute, 15
real-life combat (Battle of Midway), 11
safety gear, 13
soldier profile, 19
Special Forces, 5, 17
U.S. Air Force, 17
U.S. Army, 4, 16, 17
U.S. Navy, 17

The images in this book are reproduced through the courtesy of: Oleg Zabielin, front cover (left), p. 9; United States Department of Defense/ DVIDS, front cover (top right, bottom right), pp. 5, 6-7, 8, 9, 10, 10-11, 12, 13, 14, 15, 16, 16-17, 18, 19, 20, 21; United States Department of Defense/ Wikipedia, pp. 7, 11 (top).